JUST IN TIME!

CHILDREN'S SERMONS

Other *Just in Time!* books

Advent, Christmas, and Epiphany Services
Wedding Services
Palm Sunday and Holy Week Services
Advent Services
Baptism Services, Sermons, and Prayers
Communion Services
Pastoral Prayers for the Hospital Visit
Pastoral Prayers in Public Places
Lenten Services
Prayers and Liturgies of Confession and Assurance
Prayers for Lent and Holy Week (forthcoming)

JUST IN TIME!

CHILDREN'S SERMONS

Edited by
Anne E. Streaty Wimberly

Abingdon Press
Nashville

Library of Congress Cataloging-in-Publication Data

Children's sermons / edited by Anne E. Streaty Wimberly.
        p.   cm.—(Just in time!)
    Includes bibliographical references and index.
    ISBN 978-1-4267-0650-9 (binding: book—pbk./trade pbk., adhesive perfect binding: alk. paper) 1. Children's sermons. 2. Sermons, American. I. Wimberly, Anne Streaty, 1936-
    BV4315.C56 2010
    252'.53—dc22

                                                                                2010012554

10 11 12 13 14 15 16 17 18 19—10 9 8 7 6 5 4 3 2 1

MANUFACTURED IN THE UNITED STATES OF AMERICA

CONTENTS

Contents

Contributors: Brant D. Baker, Joyce S. Fong, Delia Halverson, Randy Hammer, Paula Hoffman, Jeff Hutcheson, Adlene Kufarimai, Bob Sharman, Anne E. Streaty Wimberly, Barbara Younger

INTRODUCTION

People were bringing little children to him in order that he might touch them; and the disciples spoke sternly to them. But when Jesus saw this, he was indignant and said to them, "Let the little children come to me; do not stop them, for it is to such as these that the kingdom of God belongs. Truly I tell you, whoever does not receive the kingdom of God as a little child will never enter it." And he took them up in his arms, laid his hands on them, and blessed them.
—Mark 10:13-16

This book is a toolbox of children's sermons that present special ways to include children in our Sunday worship and to build their faith. This toolbox brings back and adds to many of the sermons appearing in the three volumes of *The Abingdon Children's Sermon Library*. The book takes seriously the view that children belong with us in the worshiping congregation and they come with deep spiritual stirrings and yearnings that call for response. In using these sermons in worship, we recognize that Jesus welcomed children and highlighted the vital importance of their presence before God and in the community. We act on the value of children Jesus taught the disciples as we include them and give attention to them in the gathered faith community today. We show by our inclusion and attention that our children belong and that they are worthy of joining in the central thrust of worship, which is praising and honoring God.

When we include and address children in worship through sermons, we also recognize that they come with spiritual quests or yearnings. In fact, there is heightened awareness on the part of children's ministry researchers that our young have a deep spiritual yearning that goes beyond the values and material things to which they are exposed daily through technological and commercial sector marketing and offers.[1] Studies show that, as spiritual seekers, elementary-age children and those entering and in adolescence quest for:

- A *relationship with God*, the Transcendent Other.
- A sense of *the valued self* in the form of an affirmation of their worth or "somebody-ness";
- An experience of *the collective self* found in a positive sense of belonging and relationship in family and community;
- An encounter with *the guided self* communicated in an ethical framework for a faithful walk with God; and
- Readiness to be *the giving self* built through awareness of ways of caring, giving, and serving in response to love of God and neighbor.[2]

Addressing this yearning means taking seriously the opportunities sermons give to introduce children to the center of the Christian faith, which is God through Jesus Christ, and the role of Scripture in our faith formation. It suggests that we provide in sermon form helpful pathways to their faith formation that invite them to visualize and become involved firsthand in building the valued self and collective self. This calls for sermons that focus on God's view of them, the nature of the body of Christ as partners with them on the faith journey, and the role of Holy Communion, baptism, and symbols of the faith that draw them near to God and one another. Responding to the spiritual quests of children also means utilizing sermons centered on a faithful walk with God and concrete responses to faith that make their giving selves come alive. Reaching our children in worship in all these ways takes seriously our task of building their faith.

Although the sermons are provided especially for use in Sunday worship, they are well suited for use in other intergenerational gatherings of the congregation such as special seasonal and other services, as well as small- or large-group and family-focused meetings and retreats. It is understood as essential to include and give attention to children in worship and other intergenerational gatherings. However, leaders of children's church experiences may also find the sermons helpful.

How the Sermons Are Organized

The sermons are organized in two sections. Part One includes sermons focused on "The Center of Our Faith." This opening section includes sermons that center on God, Jesus Christ, the Holy Spirit, and the Bible as the church's Book.

Part Two is titled "Pathways to Our Faith." Sermons in this section engage children in exploring the nature of the community of faith; two primary sacraments of the Christian faith, Holy Communion (The Lord's Supper) and baptism; and symbols of the faith.

Preparing to Engage the Children

Children are active participants who require our engagement with their feeling, doing, watching, and thinking selves. For this reason, the sermons include ideas for dialogue, prompts, and experiences designed for children to be part of both the action and the message. You will find actual sample responses to questions that give indications of what children might say; or these sample responses may be used as prompts for their response if needed. At the same time, do not be afraid of moments of silence, because this often is a sign that children are thinking about what to say. In a number of instances, the congregation is invited to participate in the action and message as a means of making concrete our intent to stir up the children's and congregation's awareness of their life together as Christians.

It is critical that the sermons be used only as guides or tools for use with children. They are not intended to be read or followed verbatim. Preparing to use a sermon in the toolbox requires our taking the time to read through it and the Scripture reference with the goal of becoming familiar and comfortable with what they convey to the extent that we envision our own way of presenting the sermon to the children in our particular congregation. This means that we have our children in mind as we gain familiarity with the sermon material and decide on its use. Don't hesitate to use the sermons as frameworks within which to add creative ideas or as bases on which to form new sermons that respond to specific circumstances and needs. Be spontaneous!

In order to guide the flow of the sermon and free our spontaneity, a good preparatory approach is to create ahead of time an outline or some notes on steps to take—as simple or elaborate as needed. It also helps to practice aloud the steps we envision. Most of all, our preparation *is sure* when we know *for sure* the direction we need to go in a sermon and we set ourselves forward to enjoy our connection with the children and our role in their lives.

So, let's get ready! Let's be part of building children's faith!

Anne Streaty Wimberly, Editor

NOTES

1. See Katherine Turpin, "Princess Dreams: Children's Spiritual Formation in Consumer Culture" and Mary Elizabeth Moore, "Yearnings, Hopes and Visions: Youth Dreams and Ministry Futures," in Mary Elizabeth Moore and Almeda M. Wright, eds., *Children, Youth and Spirituality in a Troubling World* (St. Louis: Chalice Press, 2008), 45, 108-10; Brendan Hyde, *Children and Spirituality: Searching for Meaning and Connectedness* (London and Philadelphia: Jessica Kingsley Publishers, 2008), 138; and Joyce Ann Mercer, *Welcoming Children: A Practical Theology of Childhood* (St. Louis: Chalice Press, 2005), 31-32.

2. Brendan Hyde, *Children and Spirituality*, 130-38; and Mary Elizabeth Moore, "Yearnings, Hopes and Visions," 110-18.

Part One
The Center of Our Faith

Remember your creator in the days of your youth.
—*Ecclesiastes 12:1a*

The children's sermons in Part One highlight the importance of the relationship of our young with God. The purpose is to provide building blocks for young people's faith in God needed by them along life's journey. The opening sermons help build this relationship by focusing on praising God as the key activity of worship. The follow-up sermons invite children's view of God as Creator, real, everywhere, and as the One who made us, loves us, and helps us even when we hurt or are in trouble. The sermons also present Jesus, who loves and welcomes children, as the Bread of Life, and calls them to come into his presence and go out to tell others about him. Sermons on the Bible as the church's Book and its importance in living the way of God close this section.

Let Everything That Breathes Praise the Lord (Part One)

Scripture: Psalm 150

Season/Sunday: Any. Note that this is the first in a three-part series, but it is not necessary that the three parts be done on successive Sundays.

Focus: Anybody can praise God. We can praise God *anytime* we want. We can praise God with *anybody* we want. We can praise God *anywhere* we want. We can praise God in *any way* we want. Let everything that breathes praise the Lord.

Experience: The children will learn the different ways we can praise God. In this sermon, they will use musical instruments.

Arrangements: You will need an assortment of musical instruments, such as tambourines, triangles, and drumsticks. Even whistles, pots and pans, and other types of noisemakers will do. Make sure you have enough for each child. A narrator or reader to say the verses from Psalm 150 will keep you free to direct the "orchestra."

Leader:	Hello! Wow, what a beautiful day to praise the Lord! Let everything that breathes praise the Lord! Praise, praise, praise. I love praising the Lord. Children, what do you think it means to praise the Lord?
Children:	Worship. Praise. Praying. Singing.

Leader: Those are all great answers! Praising God is how we thank God for all that God has done for us. It is a way for us to say something good about God like, "Wow, God. You are so good and powerful." But let me ask you a question: *When* is it okay to praise the Lord?

Children: In the morning? Anytime?

Leader: Yes, we can praise God in the morning, at night, even in our dreams! And *who* can praise the Lord?

Children: People. Kids. Parents.

Leader: Those are all great answers—and not only people, but the Bible says the animals, the plants, everything that has breath should praise the Lord! Okay, *where* can we praise the Lord?

Children: In church. At home.

Leader: That's right! We can praise God here in this sanctuary. We can praise the Lord in our homes. We can praise in the park, or at the dinner table, or even at school. God invites us to praise anywhere and everywhere! Okay, last question: *How* do we praise the Lord? What are some things we do here at church and at home to praise the Lord?

Children: Sing. Pray. Preaching.

Leader: Yes! There are many ways we can praise the Lord! But there is one way you didn't mention—by playing instruments! (*Bring out your bag of instruments.*) I just happen to have a bag here full of things that will help us praise God. Let's see what we have in here. (*Take out instruments and begin to distribute. It's probably not helpful to try to keep everyone quiet as they receive their instrument, and in fact not really necessary!*) Let's praise God with these instruments. Does everyone have one? All right, let's have a concert of praising God. When I give you this signal, start playing (*show them the signal you will use*); and when I give you this signal (*show signal*), stop. Is everyone ready? Let's practice (*do a few starts and stops*). Wow, you are fast learners! I bet God can't wait to hear us praise God with our music. Okay, here we go.

Narrator: "Praise [God] with trumpet sound."

Leader: (*Signal children to play a few moments, then stop.*)

Narrator: "Praise [God] with lute and harp!"

Leader: (*Signal start and stop.*)

Narrator: "Praise [God] with tambourine and dance."

Leader: (*Signal start and stop.*)

Narrator: And "praise him with strings and pipe!"

Leader: (*Signal start and stop.*)

Narrator: "Praise [God] with clanging cymbals;...with loud clashing cymbals!"

Leader: (*Signal start and let the "music" continue for a bit longer this time, then signal to stop.*) This was really great! Let's have a prayer and give thanks that God received all of that and all our praise, and that we can give praise in so many ways. (*Prayer*)

Joyce S. Fong

(*The Abingdon Children's Sermon Library*, vol. 1, ed. Brant D. Baker © 2006 by Abingdon Press. Adapted and used by permission.)

LET EVERYTHING THAT BREATHES PRAISE THE LORD (PART TWO)

Scripture: Psalm 150

Season/Sunday: Any. Note that this is the second in a three-part series, but it is not necessary that the three parts be done on successive Sundays.

Focus: Anybody can praise God. We can praise God *anytime* we want. We can praise God with *anybody* we want. We can praise God *anywhere* we want. We can praise God in *any way* we want. Let everything that breathes praise the Lord.

Experience: The children will learn the different ways we can praise God. In this sermon they will use their bodies.

Arrangements: None are needed, but be sure you are familiar with the hand motions you will use.

Leader:	Good morning! Today we're going to continue to look at the different ways we can praise God. Do you remember when we can praise God, who can praise God, where we can praise God, and how we can praise God?
Children:	Anytime, anyone, everywhere, and with noisy instruments!
Leader:	Those are all the right answers! The Bible tells us that everyone, everywhere, can praise God at any time in just about every way! Today we're going to learn

another way we can praise God: through the movements of our bodies. Psalm 150:4 says, "Praise [God] with…dance." Everybody stand up, and let's start our dance by reaching for God (*start with your hands open and down beside your body, then raise your hands up high, like you're reaching for the sky*).

Children: (*Follow motion.*)

Leader: Now let's show with our bodies how to receive God's blessing. (*Bring your hands down to your shoulder level, stretched outward like a cross.*)

Children: (*Follow motion.*)

Leader: Now let's bring God's blessing into our hearts. (*Swoop hands together and clasp out in front of yourself, then bring the hands to the heart.*)

Children: (*Follow motion.*)

Leader: Now let's thank God for God's blessing. (*Bring your hands away from your heart to a position of prayer. You may want to kneel down.*)

Children: (*Follow motion.*)

Leader: Last, let's share this blessing with everyone. (*Swoop hands back out from the prayer position and spread outward from the body toward the congregation or one another.*)

Children: (*Follow motion.*)

Leader: Wow, that was great! That was beautiful praising. Let's invite the congregation to be involved too. (*Invite congregation to stand, and, together with children, repeat motions. Since they won't be able to kneel, you might suggest they sit instead.*)

All: (*Follow motion with leader's verbal instruction.*)

Leader: That was wonderful! Let's do that one more time, this time in silence, and have that be our closing prayer. (*Repeat sequence in silence.*)

Joyce S. Fong

(*The Abingdon Children's Sermon Library,* vol. 1, ed. Brant D. Baker © 2006 by Abingdon Press. Adapted and used by permission.)

LET EVERYTHING THAT BREATHES PRAISE THE LORD (PART THREE)

Scripture: Psalm 150

Season/Sunday: Any. Note that this is the third in a three-part series, but it is not necessary that the three parts be done on successive Sundays.

Focus: Anybody can praise God. We can praise God *anytime* we want. We can praise God with *anybody* we want. We can praise God *anywhere* we want. We can praise God in *any way* we want. Let everything that breathes praise the Lord.

Experience: The children will learn the different ways we can praise God. In this sermon they will use their voices. The sermon below also incorporates the use of instruments and bodies from the previous sermons of the series.

Arrangements: You will need to supply the instruments as you did in part 1, and it would again be helpful to have a narrator to do the reading.

Leader:	Good morning, and what a great day for everything that has breath to praise the Lord! We've been learning some of the ways to praise God—what have been your favorites so far?
Children:	Making noise!

8

Leader:	Well, I thought so! But did you know that even if you don't have anything to make noise with, and even if you can't use your body, there is something else you can use? Do you know what it is?
Children:	Our hands? Our selves? Our voices?
Leader:	That's right, our voices are another way to praise God! Let's try that; everyone repeat after me, "Let everything that breathes…"
Children:	"Let everything that breathes…"
Leader:	"Praise the Lord!"
Children:	"Praise the Lord!"
Leader:	"Let everything that breathes praise the Lord!"
Children:	"Let everything that breathes praise the Lord!"
Leader:	Awesome! Well, today we get to put together all the ways we've learned to praise God. So first of all, here are the instruments again—everyone take one (*distribute*), and remember that this is the signal to start (*show signal from part 1*), and this is the signal to stop (*show signal*). Okay, to start this we don't need our instruments, so let's put those all down and be ready to use our bodies.
Narrator:	"Praise the Lord!"
L & C:	(*Bring hands up to the sky.*)
Narrator:	"Praise God in [the] sanctuary."
L & C:	(*Bring hands to the side like a cross.*)
Narrator:	"Praise [the Lord] in [the] mighty firmament!"
L & C:	(*Bring hands to the heart.*)
Narrator:	"Praise [God] for his mighty deeds."
L & C:	(*Bring hands to prayer position and kneel down.*)
Narrator:	"Praise [the Lord] according to his surpassing greatness!"
L & C:	(*Bring hands outward to share blessings with everyone.*)
Narrator:	Now repeat after me: "Let everything that breathes…"
L & C:	"Let everything that breathes…"
Narrator:	"Praise the Lord!"
L & C:	"Praise the Lord!"

Narrator: "Let everything that breathes praise the Lord!"

L & C: "Let everything that breathes praise the Lord!"

Narrator: "Praise the Lord!"

L & C: "Praise the Lord!"

Narrator: "Praise [God] with trumpet sound;...with lute and harp!"

Leader: (*Signal children to pick up instruments and play a few moments, then stop.*)

Narrator: "Praise [God] with tambourine and dance...with strings and pipe!"

Leader: (*Signal start and stop.*)

Narrator: "Praise [God] with clanging cymbals...with loud clashing cymbals!"

Leader: (*Signal start and let the "music" continue for a bit longer this time, then signal to stop.*) Let's do that again, and have that be our prayer of praise to God today. (*Signal music to start again, and let continue for as long as you can stand it!*) Amen!

Joyce S. Fong

(*The Abingdon Children's Sermon Library*, vol. 1, ed. Brant D. Baker © 2006 by Abingdon Press. Adapted and used by permission.)

GOD CREATED EVERYTHING: AND GOD SAW THAT IT WAS GOOD!

Scripture: Excerpts from Genesis 1:1–2:3

Season/Sunday: Any, although the sermon would be particularly appropriate for an Earth Day celebration.

Focus: The sermon will help children identify that God is all around us, revealed in creation.

Experience: The children will appreciate and experience the Creation story by using all their senses to act out the story.

Arrangements: You will need a Bible, a narrator, a copy of the script below, and the awareness of the wonderful creation around you! Be sure the narrator and the leader practice the script together at least once or twice. The timing is important. The leader will guide the children in doing all the hand motions. You may choose to modify them; do whatever is natural to the leader and the children. Be "creative"!

Leader: Hello, everybody! This is the day that God has made, and God sees that it is good! Today I have a glorious story to share with you. It is the very first story from the Bible, from the book of Genesis (*hold* *the Bible up for all the children to see and open to Genesis).* It is a story about God's creation.

Narrator: "In the beginning when God created the heavens and the earth, the earth was a formless void and darkness covered the face of the deep, while a wind from God swept over the face of the waters."

Leader: Let's wave our arms back and forth and blow like the wind. (*Leader and children do the motions.*)

Narrator: "Then God said, 'Let there be light'; and there was light. And God saw that the light was good; and God separated the light from the darkness."

Leader: Ooh, that light is bright; let's put on our sunglasses. (*Leader and children pretend to put on their sunglasses.*)

Narrator: "God called the light Day, and the darkness he called Night. And there was evening and there was morning, the first day."

Leader: (*Hold up one finger for the first day. For each "evening" and "morning" throughout, leader and children act as if going to sleep and then waking up.*)

Narrator: "And God said, 'Let there be a dome in the midst of the waters, and let it separate the waters from the waters.' So God made the dome and separated the waters that were under the dome from the waters that were above the dome. And it was so. God called the dome Sky."

Leader: Let's stretch out our hands and reach for the skies. (*Leader and children do the motions.*)

Narrator: "And there was evening and there was morning, the second day."

Leader: (*Hold up two fingers for the second day; do sleep and wake-up motions.*)

Narrator: "And God said, 'Let the waters under the sky be gathered together into one place, and let the dry land appear.' And it was so. God called the dry land Earth...'"

Leader: (*Leader and children flatten hands and spread them as if flattening land.*)

Narrator:	"And the waters that were gathered together he called Seas."
Leader:	(*Wave hands up and down.*)
All:	"**And God saw that it was good.**" (*From here on, say, "And God saw that it was good," with the narrator.*)
Narrator:	"Then God said, 'Let the earth put forth vegetation: plants yielding seed, and fruit trees of every kind on earth that bear fruit with the seed in it.' And it was so. The earth brought forth vegetation: plants yielding seed of every kind, and trees of every kind bearing fruit with the seed in it."
Leader:	Mmmm…let's grab some broccoli, carrots, and spinach. Let's pick some apples and oranges from these trees. (*Leader and children pretend to pick the vegetables and fruit.*)
All:	"**And God saw that it was good.**"
Narrator:	"And there was evening and there was morning, the third day."
Leader:	(*Hold up three fingers for the third day. Sleep/wake motions.*)
Narrator:	"And God said, 'Let there be lights in the dome of the sky to separate the day from the night; and let them be for signs and for seasons and for days and years, and let them be lights in the dome of the sky to give light upon the earth.' And it was so."
Leader:	Who can show me the sun shining brightly? Good thing we have our sunglasses on!
All:	"**And God saw that it was good.**"
Narrator:	"And there was evening and there was morning, the fourth day."
Leader:	(*Hold up four fingers for day four. Sleep/wake motions.*)
Narrator:	"And God said, 'Let the waters bring forth swarms of living creatures, and let birds fly above the earth across the dome of the sky.'"
Leader:	Let's flap our wings, fly, and look down on God's creation. (*Leader and children act it out.*)

Narrator: "So God created the great sea monsters and every living creature that moves, of every kind, with which the waters swarm, and every winged bird of every kind."

Leader: Let me see some sharks, dolphins, whales, frogs, and crabs. (*Leader and children act it out.*)

All: **"And God saw that it was good."**

Narrator: "God blessed them, saying, 'Be fruitful and multiply and fill the waters in the seas, and let birds multiply on the earth.' And there was evening and there was morning, the fifth day."

Leader: (*Hold up five fingers for day five. Sleep/wake motions.*)

Narrator: "And God said, 'Let the earth bring forth living creatures of every kind: cattle and creeping things and wild animals of the earth of every kind.' And it was so. God made the wild animals of the earth of every kind, and the cattle of every kind, and everything that creeps upon the ground of every kind."

Leader: Let me see all the different land animals, like tigers, giraffes, lions, bears, squirrels, cows, and pigs. (*Leader and children act it out.*)

All: **"And God saw that it was good."**

Narrator: "Then God said, 'Let us make humankind in our image, according to our likeness; and let them have dominion over the fish of the sea, and over the birds of the air, and over the cattle, and over all the wild animals of the earth, and over every creeping thing that creeps upon the earth.' So God created humankind in his image, in the image of God he created them; male and female he created them. God blessed them."

Leader: (*While the narrator is saying the previous lines, point to yourself and one another for humankind.*)

All: **"And God saw that it was good."**

Narrator: "And there was evening and there was morning, the sixth day."

Leader: (*Hold up six fingers for day six. Sleep/wake motions.*)

Narrator: "Thus the heavens and the earth were finished, and all their multitude. And on the seventh day God finished the work that he had done, and he rested on the seventh day from all the work that he had done. So God blessed the seventh day and hallowed it, because on it God rested from all the work that he had done in creation."

Leader: (*Fold arms on chest and appear satisfied with a big sigh, sit down, and rest!*)

Leader: Isn't the story of Creation wonderful? I hope you enjoyed it as much as I did! It reminds us of how everything was made, and that God is all around us. Let us have a prayer and give thanks for all creation, asking God to help us take care of it. (*Prayer*)

Joyce S. Fong

(*The Abingdon Children's Sermon Library, vol. 1*, ed. Brant D. Baker © 2006 by Abingdon Press. Adapted and used by permission.)

GOD IS REAL

Scripture: Psalm 115:3-7
Season/Sunday: Any
Focus: God is real and alive, and working in our lives.
Experience: To celebrate and give praise for God's realness. To experience the difference between something manufactured and "the real thing."
Arrangements: You will need a toy dog (or some other stuffed animal of your choice). A helper to assist in reading the verses from Psalm 115 will help free you to concentrate on the hand motions.

Leader:	(*Carrying the toy pet with you as you greet the children*) Hello! I'd like you to meet my pet doggie, Chewy (*gently petting the dog as if it were real*). I love my little Choo-choo. She's so sweet.
Children:	(*Giggles*)
Leader:	She doesn't eat much, and she hardly ever barks. I love my dog.
Children:	That's not a real dog.
Leader:	It's not?!
Children:	No.
Leader:	Why not?
Children:	'Cause it can't bark. It can't run.
Leader:	Well, you have a good point there, and you're right: this isn't a real dog. I was showing you this because sometimes people make a statue or some kind of carving and worship it as though it were a real god and had real powers. But the God we worship is a

real God. The Bible teaches us that God is real and loves us and can really do things on our behalf. In the Bible there is a description of our real living God. Our helper,_____, is going to read from Psalm 115 (*author paraphrase*) while we do some hand motions together. Let's stand up; in fact, let's have the whole congregation stand up, and then you do what I do!

Helper: "Our God is in the heavens, and does whatever he pleases. But the people of the world have idols; idols made of things people think have value. These idols have mouths, but they can't speak."

L & C: (*Open and close mouths as if trying to say something.*)

Helper: "They have eyes, but they can't see."

L & C: (*Put hands out in front as if groping in the dark.*)

Helper: "They have ears, but they do not hear."

L & C: (*Cup hand behind ear as if trying to hear.*)

Helper: "They have noses, but they can't smell."

L & C: (*Sniff the air, and shrug shoulders in defeat.*)

Helper: "They have hands, but they can't clap."

L & C: (*Try to clap but miss.*)

Helper: "They have feet, but they can't walk."

L & C: (*Pulling up on legs as if trying to make them move.*)

Helper: "They can't even make a noise in their throats."

L & C: (*Put hand to throat and open mouth but with no sound.*)

Leader: Wow! Would you want to worship a god like that?

Children: No!

Leader: Me neither! Let's pray to our God, who is real, and who really hears us and speaks to us and loves us. (*Prayer*)

Jeff Hutcheson

WHERE IS GOD?

Scripture: Psalm 139:7-12

Season/Sunday: Any

Focus: One of our beliefs is in God's omnipresence. While this is an abstract concept beyond the capabilities of most of our children, the focus of this sermon is to have fun with it and plant the seeds for later understanding.

Experience: To search the inside of the church for God!

Arrangements: None are needed.

Leader:	Good to see everyone today! I have a question to ask: Where is God?
Children:	Up in the sky.
Leader:	Up in the sky. Anywhere else? Is God here?
Children:	Yes. God is everywhere!
Leader:	If God is everywhere, then God is here too, right? Where?
Children:	Here!
Leader:	Where?
Children:	Here!
Leader:	Well, let's look and see if we can find out where God is here. Why don't some of us go look out in the pews, some of us need to go look in the choir, and some might come up here. Maybe God is in the pulpit. (*Be sure to look in and around the pulpit, to help demystify that great bulk of furniture!*) Oh, maybe we will find God in the baptismal font; let's look in there. What do you think?
Children:	Too small.

Leader: Too small. Okay, how about under the chairs over there? (*To children at back of sanctuary:*) Did you find God back there? No? Did anybody check the choir?...They look suspicious; better check 'em out. Somebody check over there underneath the piano, would you? Not there either? Well, okay, everybody, come on back here. We'll just have to sit down again and think about this. We can't find God or see God, but we know God is here. So, where is God?

Children: I know where God is...God is everywhere and invisible.

Leader: God is everywhere and invisible? I wish you'd said that earlier! My, you are clever! That's exactly right. God is here with us, but not only just here but everywhere, all the time, and that makes God pretty amazing.

Children: God's beside you.

Leader: That's right! God is beside every one of us. Well, let's talk to God and thank God for being beside all of us and everywhere. (*Prayer*)

Brant D. Baker

SPECIALLY MADE BY GOD

Scripture: Psalm 139:13-14

Season/Sunday: Any

Focus: This sermon highlights the biblical concept of each human being as specially made by God.

Experience: Children will discover that every person is made by God and special to God.

Arrangements: You will need a large doll to begin the sermon. In readiness to give to the children at the end of the sermon, write on one side of blank 3" x 5" index cards, "God made me special and beautiful!" On the other side of the cards, write "God made everyone special and beautiful!"

Leader:	(*Lifting the doll in your arms*) I have a doll with me whose name is Barbara. I call her Barb, and both Barb and I are glad you're here. Would you say "Hi!" to Barb?
Children:	Hi, Barb!
Leader:	Tell me what you see that is special about Barb.
Children:	Barb's a doll. Barb's dressed up. Barb's pretty.
Leader:	Well, I want to say to you that you are special and beautiful. You are more special and beautiful than Barbara, because God made you. God specially made you, and me, and everyone. Let's lift up our hands and look at them. What do you see?
Children:	Fingers.

Leader: We see that each of us has fingers. But if we had a close-up picture of our fingerprints, we would see that none of our fingerprints would be exactly the same. Did you know that God gives you your special fingerprints and your footprints, too, before you are born?

Children: No. Yes.

Leader: We are different in other ways too. What are some colors of our eyes?

Children: Black, brown, blue.

Leader: What are some different colors of our hair?

Children: Black, brown, red, golden.

Leader: God also gave our skin a whole array of different colors. God made us black and brown, white and pink, red and yellow. We may call ourselves God's beautiful rainbow people. The Bible tells us that God formed every detail of you and me and everyone before we were born. We are specially made. We are one of a kind. Let's say together, "Wow! That's wonderful!"

Children: Wow! That's wonderful!

Leader: I want to give you something to remind you that you are specially and beautifully made by God. (*Hold up a card.*) It is a card that says on one side, "God made *me* special and beautiful." Let's say the words "God made *me* special and beautiful!"

Children: God made *me* special and beautiful!

Leader: When you turn the card over, you will see the words "God made *everybody* special and beautiful!" Let's say the words "God made *everybody* special and beautiful!"

Children: God made *everybody* special and beautiful!

Leader: You are special, beautiful, and awesome! Let's pray together and thank God for making us one of a kind. (*Prayer*)

Anne Streaty Wimberly

God's Love Is Forever

Scripture: Psalm 136:1
Season/Sunday: Any
Focus: God's love is forever.
Experience: The children will catch bubbles and try to save them.
Arrangements: You will need a bottle of bubbles. Consider purchasing bubbles to send home with the children, with a kind warning not to open them in church.

Leader:	(*Hold up the bottle of bubbles.*) Here's something fun! What are these?
Children:	Bubbles!
Leader:	I know you are all very clever and very good at catching things. I'm going to blow bubbles. I want each of you to catch one. (*Blow lots of bubbles.*)
Children:	I got one! Here's one! I have two!
Leader:	Good work! Now I'm going to blow bubbles again. This time I want you each to catch a bubble and save it. (*Blow more bubbles. Pause for a few seconds after you stop blowing bubbles.*) Now show me your bubbles. (*If children still have bubbles left, admire them. Wait a few more seconds until all the bubbles pop.*) Does anyone have a bubble left?
Children:	No!

Leader: Bubbles are beautiful, but they last for just a moment or two. There's only one thing that lasts forever. The Bible says to give thanks to the Lord, "for God's steadfast love will last forever" (*author paraphrase*). Let's say together, "God's love lasts forever!"

All: **God's love lasts forever!**

Leader: We can have a bubble for just a little while, but...

All: **God's love lasts forever!**

Leader: Flowers fade and tadpoles turn into frogs, but...

All: **God's love lasts forever!**

Leader: Toys get broken and sometimes even the things we love the most on this earth get taken from us, but...

All: **God's love lasts forever!**

Leader: Let's say a prayer celebrating God and God's forever love. (*Prayer*)

Barbara Younger

(*The Abingdon Children's Sermon Library*, vol. 2, ed. Brant D. Baker © 2007 by Abingdon Press. Adapted and used by permission.)

Manna from Heaven

Scripture: Exodus 16:1-16

Season/Sunday: Any

Focus: God provides for our every need, even when we do not expect it, sometimes in the least likely places and most unusual ways.

Experience: To follow Moses into the wilderness and hear the grumbling of the people, to get a chance to grumble ourselves, and then to experience God's manna from heaven.

Arrangements: You will need wrapped cookies or candy that the choir or some other group can toss out to the children. If your church prohibits eating in the sanctuary, give the children a gentle reminder at the end of the sermon to enjoy their snack later. If your choir is not in a location convenient for this, pick another section of the congregation and give them the treats and instructions beforehand.

Also, you will need to prepare several members of the congregation to be the complainers, with lines such as, *"We're hungry! When are we going to get something to eat?" "Are we there yet?" "I want to go back to Egypt! At least we had something to eat back there!"*

Finally, as the children come forward, invite the congregation to help with this sermon. Instruct them to be ready to grumble on cue. Practice the "grumbling" once or twice so they will get into the spirit of things.

> **Leader:** Hello! It's great to be together today! Today, we're going to remember the story of Moses as he led the people of God in the wilderness. Have

	you ever been on a trip where it took a really long, long, long, long, long, long, long time to get to where you were going?
Children:	Yeah! We rode in the car for hours and hours!
Leader:	Did you like riding in the car so long? Did you get grumpy?
Children:	Yes. No.
Leader:	Let's pretend we're the people of God, and we are going to follow Moses on a long journey. Come on (*start a long, slow journey around the sanctuary*). The people of God had to go on a long, long, long trip once. When God freed them from being slaves in Egypt, they had to find a new home. So they were traveling to their new home that God had promised. They had to travel through a pretty tough place called the wilderness. Do you know what they felt like sometimes?
Children:	Were they hungry? Did they get bored? Did they wonder how much farther they had to go?
Leader:	Yep. They wondered if they were ever going to get there. And they got hungry, and tired, and cranky. They began to grumble (*cue the congregation to start grumbling*) . . . and grumble . . . and complain about everything (*cue the complainers*).
Complainers:	"We're hungry! When are we going to get something to eat?" "Are we there yet?" "I want to go back to Egypt! At least we had something to eat back there!"
Leader:	(*Stopping in front of the designated spot where manna is to appear. Preferably the children will have their backs to the group that will toss the manna.*) Then Moses prayed to the Lord, and God said, "I have heard their complaining." And God promised to give them something to eat. Do you know what God gave them to eat?
Children:	McDonald's? A sandwich?

Leader: God gave them manna (*cue for the manna to be tossed gently over to the children*).

Children: Cookies! Candy!

Leader: One morning, there on the surface of the wilderness, after the dew had lifted, they saw a white flaky substance that looked like frost. They could eat it. It was called manna, and your cookies (or pieces of candy) this morning are to remind us of how God provided for the people when they were hungry. Let's have a prayer and thank God for all God's good things. (*Prayer*)

Jeff Hutcheson

(*The Abingdon Children's Sermon Library, vol. 1*, ed. Brant D. Baker © 2006 by Abingdon Press. Adapted and used by permission.)

WHEN SAD THINGS HAPPEN

Scripture: Job 1:1–2:9
Season/Sunday: Any
Focus: God is with us, even when bad things happen in our lives.
Experience: The children will create a litany that the whole congregation will use.
Arrangements: Have available an easel with a large newsprint pad (or a large piece of poster board) and a marker.

Leader: Good morning! What's the weather like? What kind of day do we have today?

Children: (*Varied responses*)

Leader: It's a lovely day today; but when it's not such a nice day, we sometimes get crabby. We feel like bad things are happening to us. (*If there's bad weather in your location today: "When we have bad weather, we don't feel that things are going too well for us, do we?"*) When are some other times when we feel that things aren't going well for us? What are some of the sad things that can happen in our lives? As you mention them, I'm going to write them on this large paper so that we can all see them. (*Write responses, leaving a line at the top to write the response that is suggested below.*)

27

Children: (*Varied responses. Be sure that things like storms, divorce, death, illness, and other serious problems are mentioned.*)

Leader: These are all sad things, and most of these are things that happen even though we have nothing to do with making them happen. There is a story in the Bible about a man named Job who had some really bad things happen to him. He had lots of animals: oxen, donkeys, sheep, and camels. They were all taken from him or burned up in a fire. His servants who cared for the animals were killed. His children were killed when a great wind blew down the house where they were having a meal together. And then Job got terrible sores all over his body. Now, how do you suppose Job felt then?

Children: (*Varied responses*)

Leader: Job was very upset, but he believed in God so much that he knew God was with him in the sad times as well as the good times.

(*Point to the list.*) We've listed lots of bad things that happen in our lives, but we can know that God doesn't cause those bad things to happen specifically to us. We can know that God is sad when we are sad, and God is with us even in the sad times.

We're going to use these sad things that happen in our lives to make a litany, a kind of special prayer. I will read the list, and after each sad thing that I read, you and the congregation will respond with the words "God is with us, even at this sad time." (*Write these words at the top of the paper.*)

Leader: (*Read from the list:*) In a hurricane . . .

All: (*Prompt the children and congregation to respond:*) **God is with us, even at this sad time.**

Leader: In illness . . .

All: **God is with us, even at this sad time.**

Leader: (*Continue down the list. Close the litany with a prayer giving thanks for God's presence even in sad times.*)

Delia Halverson

(*The Abingdon Children's Sermon Library*, vol. 2, ed. Brant D. Baker © 2007 by Abingdon Press. Adapted and used by permission.)

Jesus Loves Children

Scripture: Mark 10:13-16

Season/Sunday: Any

Focus: Jesus has a special love for children, welcomes them, and wants others to see not simply his welcome of them but the qualities of respect, trust, humility, and enthusiasm about life children show that he wants others to model and use in carrying out God's work in the world.

Experience: The children will hear and respond to the telling of the story found in the Gospel of Mark about Jesus' welcome of a child. Each child will also say her name or his name aloud and will then hear the response of the whole congregation: "Jesus loves you."

Arrangements: Have the Bible in readiness to show that the story being told in your own words comes from the Bible. Also be ready to close with the song "Jesus Loves Me, This I Know." Seek help from the choir if needed.

Leader:	Hello! How is everyone today? I have a special story to share with you today about Jesus' love of children and Jesus' love of you. But before I tell it, I want to ask you two questions. My first question is: Who brought you here today?
Children:	My mother! My grandmother! My parents!
Leader:	That's great! My next question is: Why did they bring you here?
Children:	They wanted me to be with them. They wanted me to learn about God. I don't know.

30

Leader: I see. Well, in the beginning of the story in the New Testament book of Mark in the Bible (*opening the Bible*), people were bringing children to Jesus because they wanted this very special man called Jesus to touch them and bless them. But do you know what happened?

Children: (*Various responses*)

Leader: You might be surprised to know that some of Jesus' followers started saying, "Move back! Don't come here! Get away! Can't you see that Jesus doesn't have time for you? He has more important things to do!" So, what do you suppose happened then?

Children: (*Various responses*)

Leader: The children and those who brought them might have felt bad and started to leave. But Jesus didn't stop the children. He stopped his followers and said with a strong, demanding voice, "Let the little children come to me; do not stop them; for it is to such as these that the kingdom of God belongs." Wasn't that a great thing Jesus did?

Children: Yes!

Leader: Jesus spoke out to his followers because he loved children; and that hasn't changed. Jesus loves each one of you and will never turn you away. But he also had a message to anyone who thinks Jesus should not welcome you in his presence. He let his followers know that there is something about the way children are—about the way you are—that others should be like in order to carry out God's work in the world. Jesus was talking about the respect children show others that all Christians should show God. Jesus was also talking about your trust in others that all Christians should have in God and the happiness you have and show that God wants to see in those who follow Jesus. I would like all of us to remember that Jesus loves children and loves you. I would like each of you to say your name as loudly as you can, and after each name is said, let's have the whole congregation say aloud, "Jesus loves you!"

All: (*Each child says her name or his name aloud, followed by the congregation's response, "Jesus loves you!"*)

Leader: Let's close with everyone singing the song "Jesus Loves Me, This I Know."

Anne Streaty Wimberly

JESUS IS THE BREAD OF LIFE

Scripture: Matthew 15:32-39

Season/Sunday: Any, but Sunday when Holy Communion is being served would be most appropriate.

Focus: Jesus as the Bread of Life, the one who satisfies the hunger inside us.

Experience: As the children distribute the "bread and fish," they will be made to feel like Jesus' disciples, as well as be given a taste of service.

Arrangements: Beforehand, secure enough small, inexpensive baskets so that each child will have one. Also secure a sufficient number of fish-shaped crackers so that every worshiper can take one. (Have a good supply to spare—you don't want to run out of food while reenacting this miracle story!) Divide the fish-shaped crackers into the baskets. If the church is large, or the children particularly young, it might be a good idea to have adult ushers ready to help in the logistics of the distribution. Finally, as the children distribute the baskets of fish-shaped crackers, an appropriate hymn such as "Break Thou the Bread of Life" may be played (or sung).

Leader:	Good morning! Have you ever been away from home, perhaps shopping at the mall or watching a parade or on a fishing trip, or maybe even at church, when you got really hungry?
Children:	Yes!

Leader:	Most of us have done that. Well, often when Jesus was teaching the people, they would walk for miles to hear him teach and time would get away from them so that before long they realized they were hungry and had not brought anything to eat. Jesus felt sorry for the people and did what he could to feed them. In one of those stories, the writer of Matthew's Gospel tells about a crowd of people who had been with Jesus three days and had nothing left to eat. Matthew wants to teach us in this story that Jesus is the Bread of Life. Can you say that with me?
L & C:	**Jesus is the Bread of Life!**
Leader:	Jesus' disciples were able to come up with seven loaves of bread and a few small fish. Who is Jesus?
Children:	**Jesus is the Bread of Life!**
Leader:	By breaking and breaking and breaking the seven loaves of bread and a few small fish into smaller and smaller pieces, Jesus was able to see that all the people were given something to eat. Who is Jesus?
Children:	**Jesus is the Bread of Life!**
Leader:	Then the disciples gave the bread and the fish to all the people. And today you get to be Jesus' disciples too! Can you make sure that everyone here this morning gets a piece of bread, because...
Children:	**Jesus is the Bread of Life!**
Leader:	(*Begin distributing baskets and sending children out for the distribution while you continue talking.*) You may notice that our bread today (*hold up a fish-shaped cracker*) is in the form of a fish. It is thought that the fish was the earliest symbol used by Christians to let others know they were followers of Jesus, and let's all say it together (*inviting congregation as well*), because...
All:	**Jesus is the Bread of Life!**
Leader:	(*As the distribution is winding down*) After feeding all the people, the disciples brought the baskets back

(*signal children to return*). The disciples saw that they
had leftovers! Because...

All: **Jesus is the Bread of Life!**

Leader: The early followers of Jesus saw in this miracle a spiritual lesson: Jesus satisfies the spiritual hunger and
spiritual searching that is inside every one of us.
Because...

All: **Jesus is the Bread of Life!**

Leader: All of us have an inner hunger, a hunger of the
heart, to know God, to learn God's ways, to live like
God wants us to live. And Jesus is the one who satisfies that hunger, as he shows us who God is, as he
teaches us God's ways, and as he instructs us on how
to best live our lives. Because...

All: **Jesus is the Bread of Life!**

Leader: (*Make this refrain the closing prayer by simply adding,
"Amen!" or offer closing prayer.*)

Randy Hammer

JESUS CALLS US TO COME (AND GO)

Scripture: Matthew 4:18-22 (NLT)

Season/Sunday: Any

Focus: Jesus' invitation to us as his disciples is an invitation into a relationship in order that we may see who he is and seek to be like him. Just as he invited those first disciples to come into a partnership, so he still calls and invites us to come to him today. Of course, eventually in the Gospel narrative Jesus also tells the disciples to go. That might not feel like a relational gesture, but he has a reason for it; and even as he tells them to go, he promises to be with them.

Experience: The children and the leader will move around the sanctuary to experience "coming" and "going."

Arrangements: None are needed, but be sure you use the words *come* and *go* often and with lots of emphasis!

Leader:	I would like to invite the children to *come* and join me in the front of the sanctuary. I am so glad you could *come* and join me. Now that we are all settled in, I would like you all to get up and *go* to the back of the sanctuary (*direct them to a specific spot, for example, the back doors, the center aisle, or near the last pew*).
Children:	(*Move to spot indicated.*)
Leader:	You did a great job following instructions, but now you are so far away from me. Maybe I just need to

come to where you are so we will be together (*move to join children*). Now that we are all together, *come* with me to the front of the sanctuary, and let's sit down there.

Children: This is a lot of exercise!

Leader: (*As you reassemble*) Today our Bible story tells about a time when Jesus invited some people to *come* and follow him. The men were busy doing their work as fishermen, catching fish to sell in the markets. Jesus said to them, "'*Come*, be my disciples, and I will show you how to fish for people!' And they left their nets at once and went with him. A little farther up the shore he saw two other brothers, James and John, sitting in a boat with their father, Zebedee, mending their nets. And he called them to *come*, too. They immediately followed him, leaving the boat and their father behind" (Matthew 4:19-22 NLT, emphasis added).

When I told you to *come* to the front of the church, we were very close. When I told you to *go*, did it seem as if we were close?

Children: No!

Leader: When I *came* to join you in the back of the church, were we close?

Children: Yes!

Leader: So we might say that when we are invited to *come*, it is time to be close, like what Jesus did with Simon, Andrew, James, and John in our story today. Jesus invited them to *come*, and they got to be close with Jesus. When you invite friends to *come* to your house to play, you get to be close to them. When people invite you to *come* to eat, you get to be close to them. But Jesus invited the fishermen to *come* be with him, and they learned wonderful things and got to know Jesus. They learned that Jesus was the Son of God and how Jesus loved and cared for people and that coming to him meant they should care for and love people like he did. That happened because they *came* when he invited them to *come*. Did you know that Jesus still calls us to *come*? What happens when we *come* to Jesus?

Children: We get close to him!

Leader: That's right! When we *come* to Jesus and we feel ourselves in his presence, we get a little closer to him and want to be like him. And then, Jesus also asks us to *go*, to *go* out into the world, to *go* to people who need our help, to *go* and share the good news of Jesus' love and how God wants people to *come* and be like Jesus too. And it's also good news that no matter if we are *coming* or *going*, Jesus is with us! Let's have a prayer and ask Jesus to help us *come* to him every day and become more like him every day. (*Prayer*)

Paula Hoffman

(*The Abingdon Children's Sermon Library, vol. 1*, ed. Brant D. Baker © 2006 by Abingdon Press. Adapted and used by permission.)

THE NAME ABOVE EVERY NAME

Scripture: 3 John (NIV); Philippians 2:9-10 (NIV)
Season/Sunday: Any
Focus: This sermon focuses on the name of Jesus and the importance of the name.
Experience: Children will help solve the mystery of 3 John 7 by searching for the clue.
Arrangements: If your worship area has a large pulpit Bible, then you should plan to use it to solve the mystery of the name. If not, plan to carry a Bible yourself as you go out in search of the clue. Arrange ahead of time for someone to bring a study Bible with a concordance to worship. On cue, this volunteer will look up the word *name* in the concordance, and find the reference to Philippians 2:9-10, thus providing the clue. A cape and magnifying glass would be fun props for the leader!

Leader:	Hello, kids, I'm so glad to see you today! Today there is a mystery afoot, and I am going to need your help. Third John verse 7 says, "It was for the sake of the Name that they went out" (NIV). Will you help me find a clue to solve the mystery of the name?
Children:	Yes! Okay!
Leader:	Good. Let's think about this (*repeating verse slowly*), "It was for the sake of the Name that they went out" Aha! So they "went out." I guess that means

39

we should go out too (*get up and start walking into the worship area*). And that's the mystery, isn't it? We've got to find a clue to know what the name is. Well, what are you waiting for (*hands on hips*)? We've got a mystery to solve. Come on, we're going out to look for a clue (*motion for the kids to join you*)! (Note: *if one of the children suggests that the name might be "Jesus," cover by saying, "That could be, but we aren't sure yet!"*) Maybe we can find a clue under here (*lean down to look under an unoccupied pew or chair*). Do you think we can find out what the name is under here?

Children: (*Engage in the search.*)

Leader: Hmmm. I wonder if it is up in one of these windows?

Children: No!

Leader: Well, could it be behind your ear?

Children: (*Laughter*) No!

Leader: Well, then, we only have one more place to look. (*Turn to the congregation.*) Does anyone have a study Bible with a concordance?

Volunteer: I do!

Leader: That's great because a concordance is a list that tells us where different words are used in the Bible. (*To the volunteer:*) Will you look up the word *name* and give us a clue as to where we can look? (*Begin rubbing your hands together in delight.*) I think this is going to work, don't you?

Children: Yes!

Volunteer: The word *name* shows up in Philippians 2:9-10.

Leader: I knew it! The Bible gives us clues to help us understand the Bible! Let's look it up! (*Hurry to the pulpit Bible, or use another one.*) Here it is; repeat these words after me: "Therefore God exalted him to the highest place (*pause for echo*) and gave him the name that is above every name (*pause*), that at

40

the name of Jesus (*pause*) every knee should bow"
(Philippians 2:9-10 NIV).

So! The mystery of the name is solved!
(*Reverently:*) I think we need to kneel like the
verse says, and let's have a prayer thanking God for
the name of Jesus. (*Prayer*)

Bob Sharman

(*The Abingdon Children's Sermon Library, vol. 3*, ed. Brant D. Baker
© 2008 by Abingdon Press. Adapted and used by permission.)

WHY WE READ THE BIBLE

Scripture: Romans 12:2

Season/Sunday: Any, or Christian Education Sunday

Focus: The Bible changes our view of things; it stretches our imaginations and helps us see the world more as God sees it. The Bible is a gift that helps us fulfill the call to be transformed by the renewing of our minds. It helps us discern "what is the will of God—what is good and acceptable and perfect."

Experience: To experience a different view of the sanctuary and relate that to why we read the Bible. The Bible gives us a different view of our lives.

Arrangements: You will need a sturdy stepladder or bench that you can stand on, a helper to help you and the children stand safely on the ladder or bench, and a Bible.

Leader:	(*Standing on the ladder or bench*) Good morning! Do you know what I'm doing?
Children:	Standing on a ladder (or bench)!
Leader:	That's right. Can you guess why I am standing on this ladder (or bench)?
Children:	So you'll be taller? Just because? I don't know.
Leader:	Nope. I'm standing up here because I want to get a different view of the sanctuary today. I want to get a different way of looking at our congregation. (*Looking around*) It sure looks different from up here. You want to take a look?

Children:	I do! (*With your helper, assist as many children as are interested or as time allows to stand on the ladder or bench and take a look around.*)
Leader:	Do things look different from up there?
Children:	Yes! I can see everything.
Leader:	It changes your whole point of view, doesn't it? Can you think of any other way to get a different way of looking at things (*holding up Bible to prompt answer*)?
Children:	Stand on the Bible?
Leader:	Well, kind of. Not stand on it with our feet, but stand in it to know what it says and see things the way God sees things. That's another way of getting to see things differently. Reading the Bible is like standing on a ladder or bench, or standing on our heads. It gives us a different view of the world and ourselves. It helps us see things more the way God might see them.
Children:	Can we stand on our heads?
Leader:	Not right now. Let's pray and ask God to help us stand on the Bible to see things God's way. (*Prayer*)

Jeff Hutcheson

(*The Abingdon Children's Sermon Library, vol. 1*, ed. Brant D. Baker © 2006 by Abingdon Press. Adapted and used by permission.)

THE BIBLE SHOWS THE WAY

Scripture: Psalm 25:4
Season/Sunday: Any
Focus: The Bible helps us know how God wants us to live.
Experience: A child and an older helper will lay out a yarn path along an aisle of the church. After this is done, the leader will take the children down the path.
Arrangements: Most churches have an aisle long enough to lay out a simple yarn path. If this isn't practical, perhaps a smaller path can be laid out in the front of the church. Use thick yarn, since thinner yarn may be difficult for the child to unroll. Recruit a teen or an adult helper. Have a Bible handy from which to read the verse.

Leader:	(*Holding up the ball of yarn*) This may look like an ordinary ball of yarn, but today we're going to do something very important with it. We're going to lay out a path. I need a volunteer to lay out a path down the aisle of the church.
Children:	I will! I will!
Leader:	I'm going to let (*child's name*) help us today, along with (*helper's name*). You can make a straight path or a squiggly one down the aisle. (*The helper can hold one end of the yarn as the child unrolls it.*) While we wait for our yarn path to be made, I want you to tell me about any paths or trails you have walked.

Children: I walk on the sidewalk near my house. There is a nature path at my school. My grandma has a path to her pond.

Leader: Those all sound like wonderful paths! It looks like our yarn path is finished. Let's all follow it! (*Lead the children on the path. As you do, say things like "This is a great path," "This path helps me know how to go," "Thanks, [child's name and helper's name], for making this path." When you get to the end of the path, turn everyone around and walk the path back up to the front. Invite the children to sit down again.*) There is a verse in the Bible that talks about paths (*open the Bible and read Psalm 25:4*). The person who wrote these words was asking God to show the path of how we should live. (*Close the Bible and hold it up.*) The Bible is like a path. The words in the Bible tell us how God wants us to live. If we follow the path of the Bible, then we are following God's path. Let's all say together, "The Bible is God's path!"

Children: **The Bible is God's path!**

Leader: When we don't know which way to go, we can find out because . . .

Children: **The Bible is God's path!**

Leader: If we're lost in life, we don't need to worry because . . .

Children: **The Bible is God's path!**

Leader: Let's have a prayer thanking God for the Bible. (*Prayer; after sermon have helper roll up the yarn.*)

Barbara Younger

(*The Abingdon Children's Sermon Library, vol. 2*, ed. Brant D. Baker © 2007 by Abingdon Press. Adapted and used by permission.)

PLANTING SEEDS/GROWING GOD'S WORD IN US

Scripture: 1 Corinthians 3:6 (NIV); Luke 8:11 (NIV)
Season/Sunday: Any
Focus: The sermon focuses on the importance of God's word in Scripture.
Experience: The children will experience a visual of growing from the inside and practice a couple of foundational verses for growing.
Arrangements: None needed

Leader:	Good morning, everyone! You know, you are growing bigger all the time—look at how big you are getting. Look!
Children:	(*Look at themselves.*)
Leader:	Well, our Scripture verse for today talks about growing. It comes from 1 Corinthians 3:6. "I planted the seed," says Paul, "but God made it grow" (NIV). Wow, a seed has been planted in you! Do you feel like a seed is planted in you?
Children:	Yes. No. What kind of seed?
Leader:	Well, that was the question I was going to ask. What kind of seed could it be? Do you have a broccoli seed planted in you?

Children:	Yuck! No!
Leader:	Well, maybe there is an oak tree seed in you, or maybe a beautiful flower seed is inside you. Everybody open your mouths; let me see if there are any seeds down there.
Children:	(*Children open their mouths.*)
Leader:	Well, I don't really see any flower or broccoli seeds inside you, but Jesus once said, "The seed is the word of God" (Luke 8:11 NIV). Hmmm. If the seed is the word of God, and God is going to grow that seed, what do you think we ought to do?
Children:	I don't know. Eat more green beans?
Leader:	Do you think that maybe we should plant "seeds" of God's word into ourselves?
Children:	Yes!
Leader:	Sure, if we learn God's word, it's like putting God's word into ourselves. In fact, let's start right now to put some of God's *word-seeds* inside us, so that God can make them grow. And we can start with the two verses you just heard. I'll say them and you repeat them back. Ready? Here we go, "I planted the seed..."
Children:	"I planted the seed..."
Leader:	"But God made it grow."
Children:	"But God made it grow."
Leader:	I think those *word-seeds* from God are growing inside you already! I want you to practice these seeds again today for your families when you get home so you don't forget them. And let's have a prayer giving thanks for all God's good seed. (*Prayer*)

Optional ending

Leader:	I think those *word-seeds* from God are growing inside you already! And I think you are learning them so well that you could teach those *word-seeds* to the congregation. Let's turn around and see if we can teach them. Everybody ready? Repeat after us. (*Leader can*

prompt the children if necessary; children repeat, echoed by the congregation.)

Bob Sharman

Part Two
Pathways to Our Faith

For as in one body we have many members, and not all the members have the same function, so we, who are many, are one body in Christ, and individually we are members one of another. We have gifts that differ according to the grace given to us.
—Romans 12:4-6a

The sermons in Part Two create opportunities for children to discover themselves and the congregation they are part of as children of God and the body of Christ. The sermons are pathways for helping children see themselves and others who are big, small, men, women, old, young, from different neighborhoods, and of different cultures, groups, and colors being led by Jesus, the Head of the church, and united together to carry out the work Jesus began. The sermons also present Holy Communion (the Lord's Supper), baptism, and symbols of the Christian church as pathways for children's seeing and experiencing God's people in the presence of God and God's presence with and in us.

WE ARE THE CHILDREN OF GOD

Scripture: 1 John 3:1a
Season/Sunday: Any
Focus: This sermon focuses on the biblical concept of the children of God.
Experience: Children will discover that we are all God's children, and will lead a short litany of proclamation for and with the congregation.
Arrangements: None needed

Leader:	Hello, children of God. I want you to know that God says to call you "children of God." Would you like to see where?
Children:	Yes.
Leader:	It is right here in First John 3:1; in fact, why don't you repeat it after me? "See what love" (*pause for echo*), "the Father has given us" (*pause*), "that we should be called" (*pause*), "children of God" (*pause*); "and that is what we are." So, you are children of God. Are there any other children of God around here?
Children:	No. Yes. In the nursery.
Leader:	That's right, there are some children of God in other places in our church. But I mean right here. Are there any more children of God right here?
Children:	No. Maybe. Yes?

Leader: Well, this verse is saying that if God loves us, then we are all children of God. That is very good news, I want you to know. Let's do this (*lower your voice conspiratorially and address the children*): let's tell the rest of the congregation that they are God's children too! Will you help me?

Children: Yes!

Leader: Okay, when I say, "Who are the children of God?" you point to them and call out, "You are the children of God!" And the second time I ask, say, "We are the children of God!" Ready?

Children: Yes!

Leader: Let's stand up. Who are the children of God?

Children: (*Pointing to the congregation*) You are the children of God!

Leader: Who are the children of God?

Children: We are the children of God!

Leader: That was great! Let's do it a couple more times, but let's give the congregation a part. (*To the congregation:*) After the children answer the question, you all say, "That is what we are!" Everybody ready? Who are the children of God?

Children: (*Pointing to the congregation*) You are the children of God!

Congregation: That is what we are!

Leader: Who are the children of God?

Children: We are the children of God!

Congregation: That is what we are!

Leader: That was fantastic! Let's have a prayer and give thanks that we are all children of God. (*Prayer*)

Bob Sharman

THE BODY OF CHRIST

Scripture: Romans 12:4-5; 1 Corinthians 12:14-26; Ephesians 4:14-16

Season/Sunday: Any, but may also be used around stewardship season.

Focus: The body of Christ is the Apostle Paul's powerful image to describe the interrelated structure of the church. Each part needs the other; each part has a specific task that it is uniquely able to perform. The focus of this sermon is to explore what these different parts of the body are in a particular church.

Experience: To relate the parts of the body mentioned by Paul to specific groups within the church, by asking members of those groups to stand when they hear their group called (and its corresponding part of the body you have assigned to it). Children will be asked to stand when they see their parents or the persons they came with stand to form bridges from adult to child through church service groups.

Arrangements: You will need a list of the various parts of the body mentioned by Paul in 1 Corinthians, alongside a list of all the groups in your church. Organize the list to match your church's ministries. The list shown here is an example.

Leader: Good to see you today! I want to read to you a few verses from the Bible, from the book of Romans: "For as in one body we have many members, and not all the members have the same function, so we, who are many, are one body in Christ, and individually we are members one of another." A man named Paul wrote these words, and he is saying that a church is a lot like our bodies. Part of the church is a foot, part of it is a hand, part of it is an eye. Do you know which parts of our church are these things?

Children: No.

Leader: I thought you might not, so I made a list! (*To the congregation:*) How about standing when I call out a part of our church body that you're a member of? (*To the children:*) And how about standing when you see your folks or the one you came with stand, okay? Then here we go.

- Foot: Missions, Ministry
- Hand: Deacons or Trustees, or Administrative Officers
- Ear: Women's Groups, Men's Groups, Youth Ministry, Young Adult or Singles' Ministry
- Eye: Worship Leaders and Planners, Choir Members, Ushers, Acolytes
- Arm: Sunday School Classes
- Elbow: Christian Education leaders

(*And so on; your list can be as brief or as comprehensive as you like! It probably would be good, however, to end with the following:*) And now, will all the other parts of this body of Christ please stand?

(*To the children:*) There's one very important part of the body that I didn't mention, the Head. Who do you suppose is the Head of the church?

Children: The minister? My daddy? Jesus?

Leader: Some interesting answers, but I think I'd have to agree that Jesus is the Head of the church! Jesus is the one who tells all the other parts what to do, and then helps them do what they need to do.

Let's have a prayer, and since we're all standing up, let's all hold hands while we thank God that we are joined together in one body, with Jesus Christ as our Head. (*Prayer*)

Brant D. Baker

(*The Abingdon Children's Sermon Library*, vol. 2, ed. Brant D. Baker © 2007 by Abingdon Press. Adapted and used by permission.)

THE CHURCH PUZZLE

Scripture: 1 Corinthians 12:14-26
Season/Sunday: Any
Focus: Church is not about how we fit in, but how we fit together.
Experience: To learn something about being part of the body of Christ.
Arrangements: You will need a large-piece jigsaw puzzle. A twenty-four-piece puzzle is a good size.

Leader: Good morning! Raise your hand if you have ever put together a puzzle. (*Most all the children will raise their hands.*) Good, because I need your help. (*Pull out the puzzle.*) I brought a puzzle with me today, and I wonder if you'd help me put it together.

Children: Sure!

Leader: (*Open lid and look inside, pull out a couple of pieces and look at them.*) Oh, I see, they all fit in this box. (*Put the pieces back in.*) Well, that was easier than I thought; all the pieces are already together.

Children: No, you have to put the pieces together.

Leader: (*Surprised*) You mean they don't just go in the box?

Children: No, you put them together.

Leader: (*Take two pieces out again.*) Okay, so you take two pieces and put them together (*force the two pieces together so it is obvious they are not a match*). Like this?

Children: No, that piece doesn't go with that one. They have to fit together.

56

Leader: (*Looking at the pieces*) You're right; these two pieces don't fit together. I guess we won't need them (*toss puzzle pieces over your shoulder and reach in the box for two more*).

Children: No, don't throw them away. They go with the puzzle.

Leader: (*Retrieve the pieces.*) Oh, okay. So we need every piece.

Children: Find the pieces that fit together.

Leader: Okay, so somehow all the pieces in this box fit together.

Children: Yes. Now do you get it?

Leader: (*Find two pieces that fit together.*) Like this?

Children: Yeah.... Didn't you know how to put a puzzle together?

Leader: I like to put puzzles together! But today I wanted your help for a special reason. You see, we can learn something about church from putting together a puzzle. We are all like pieces of a puzzle (*hold up a piece*). Each one of us is unique and special. Some of us are big and others are small. Some are women and others are men. Some are young and others are old. We come from different neighborhoods. We may be different colors from different cultures or groups of people. But all of us are children of God, belonging to the church. And when we come to church, our main concern shouldn't be how we fit in, but how we fit together. We all fit together in some unique and special way. When we do, we make up the body of Jesus Christ. Should I throw away any one piece (*hold up a piece of the puzzle*)?

Children: No, you'll need it!

Leader: That's right, each and every piece is one of us, and each and every piece is needed. Each one of us is important to the body of Christ, and each one of us is special, and we all fit together in a special way. Let's pray. (*Prayer*)

Jeff Hutcheson

HOLY COMMUNION: SENSING THE WORD OF GOD

Scripture: Matthew 26:26-28 (KJV)

Season/Sunday: Holy Communion (The Lord's Supper)

Focus: The word of God comes to us in many forms. Holy Communion, also called the Lord's Supper, is one of those forms, but it is unique in its communication to us through our physical selves.

Experience: To become aware that we receive God's word in various ways and to experience that word with the full variety of our senses.

Arrangements: You will need: a Bible and a picture or other visual representation of the bread (wheat) and wine (grapes) (e.g., a stained-glass window or wood carving on the front of a table). Presumably this sermon will be used on a day when Communion is being celebrated, so the Communion table will be spread.

Leader:	Hello, everybody, good to see you today. I'd like to read to you, "Jesus...said, 'Take, eat; this is my body....Drink ye all of it; for this is my blood of the new testament'" (Matthew 26:26-28 KJV). What did we do just now?
Children:	(*A certain guilty silence!*) Read the Bible?

Leader: Well, I read the Bible. What did you do (*point to ear if the children need an added prompt*)?

Children: Listened?

Leader: Listened, that's right! You heard the word of God. Okay, let's go over there (*move to visual representation of elements*). Look up there. What's that a picture of?

Children: A cup. Some grapes. Wheat.

Leader: Right, and what are we doing right now (*point at your eyes*)?

Children: Looking?

Leader: Right! We're seeing the symbols for Communion. Great! Okay, everybody come with me up to the front. So far we've heard and we've seen. What's this (*point to Lord's Supper*)?

Children: Food?

Leader: Food, and we call this food the Lord's Supper. Later on in the service what are we going to do?

Children: Eat?

Leader: We're going to eat! God has given us so many ways to learn about God's word! We can *hear* the word of God, we can *see* the word of God, and we can *eat*— or *taste*—the word of God. And all these things are ways God has to remind us that God's word to us is that we are loved by God. Let's have a prayer and thank God for giving us all these ways to know of God's word and of God's love. (*Prayer*)

Brant D. Baker

(*The Abingdon Children's Sermon Library, vol. 3*, ed. Brant D. Baker © 2008 by Abingdon Press. Adapted and used by permission.)

WE ARE GOD'S FAMILY

Scripture: Galatians 3:28 (NLT)

Season/Sunday: World Communion Sunday

Focus: Regardless of our differences, we are one family of God. As followers of Jesus Christ, we are called to love and respect our brothers and sisters, no matter what color or part of the world they now live in or come from. An important day for celebrating our oneness as a family of God and for remembering Jesus Christ as our Head is World Communion Sunday.

Experience: Children and the congregation will sing along with "Jesus Loves the Little Children" as they take their positions. (*If possible, form a big circle around the sanctuary representing the world; or the children may be invited to come to the front.*) Preselect adults to give a short description of each continent as the children name the seven continents.

Arrangements: Have your regular World Communion Sunday setting, but add a globe or world map, have available a colorful beach ball with names of the world's continents on it, and prepare description cards for each continent with the information indicated below. Also select children to represent Christians from the different continents. The beach ball game will allow children to learn more about the world around them and the concept of World Communion Sunday. The leader will throw the ball to a child and he or she will name a continent listed on the ball followed by a selected adult's description of the identified continent. (*Repeat this until all continents are identified.*)

ASIA
It is the largest continent. It stretches east of Japan to the southeastern Arabian Peninsula. Christianity is the religion of 13.3 percent of the population.

AFRICA
It is the second-largest continent. Africa covers about 22 percent of the world's land. Regardless of other religions, Africa is 46 percent Christian.

NORTH AMERICA
It is around twice the size of Europe. It is composed of three countries: Canada, Mexico, and the United States. Eighty-five percent of the population is Christian.

SOUTH AMERICA
It is the fourth-largest continent. It has the world's largest river and longest mountain range. Ninety-three percent of the population is Christian.

ANTARCTICA
It is the sixth-largest continent and is ice-covered throughout the year. It is impossible for people to live on this continent.

EUROPE
It is the fifth-largest continent and it has a variety of minerals. In recent years, Christianity has been declining in Europe.

AUSTRALIA
It is the smallest continent. There are rare weather extremes. Australia is known for its wildlife species. The native people of Australia are called Aborigines. Sixty-three percent of the population is Christian.

Leader: (*Moving to the center of the circle or among the children*) Through the blood of Jesus Christ, we are now one family of God. We thank God for this day of celebrating Communion with our brothers and sisters around the world. Jesus gave away his life so that we might have abundant life. As we share this meal, let us remember that there are those who may be different from us. Jesus died for us all, and together we are one family of God. Before this special meal, let us explore our world and those with whom we share it. (*Throwing the beach ball to children within the circle*)

Children: (*The ball catcher names a continent he or she sees on the ball. All children repeat the name of the continent together.*)

Volunteer: (*A selected adult gives the description of the identified continent.*)

Leader: (*After all the continents have been identified*) Thank you for identifying God's family from around the world. We may be miles apart, but we are one in Jesus Christ. Around our communities we have people who may be different from us but who believe, as we do, that Jesus Christ is the living Son of God. They are part of our family. Now that you have discovered that you have so many brothers and sisters in Christ, how do you feel to be part of this family?

Children: (*Random selection; children share who they are, where they come from, and how they feel to be part of God's family.*)

Leader: We are one family. The wonderful meal on World Communion Sunday reminds us of God's love toward us through his Son, Jesus Christ. Remember the words of the Apostle Paul: "There is no longer Jew or Gentile, slave or free, male or female. For you are all Christians—you are one in Christ Jesus" (Galatians 3:28 NLT). It is through this World Communion that we celebrate our oneness in Christ. Every member of this family is important, for we are equal in the eyes of God. As you remember, ask God to give you a heart (*ask children to place their hands over their hearts*) to love those who are different from you. Let us pray. (*All join in the Lord's Prayer.*)

Adlene Kufarimai

BAPTISM: A GIFT TO CELEBRATE

Scripture: Deuteronomy 4:9-10
Season/Sunday: Baby's baptism
Focus: The church helps babies grow to be Christians
Experience: By making a baptism gift, the children will learn how the church has responsibility to help babies know God's love.
Arrangements: Purchase a square of fleece for a baby blanket (or some other item may be completed as a gift). Cut fringes on two or three sides of the blanket, leaving enough space for the children to each cut at least one fringe during the service. Provide scissors to cut the fringes of the blanket. If most of your children are preschool, ask parents or other adults to accompany the children to the front to assist with this experience.

Leader: Good morning! This is a special day for a member of our church family. Today the pastor is going to baptize [has baptized] (*Name*). Baptizing a baby holds a special meaning. It means that we recognize how God will be a part of this child throughout life. It also means that we, as a church family, will help the child know God's love. What are some ways that we can show love?

Children: (*Various responses*)

Leader: These are all good ways. I brought something today that we can make and give to the baby, and which will also show God's love. Each of you will have a chance to cut one of the fringes on the blanket. As you finish cutting your fringe, I'd like for you to say, "We love you, (*Name*), and God loves you."

Children: (*Various responses as each child cuts a fringe*)

Leader: Thank you for helping to make this blanket (*if it isn't finished, say, "I'll see that the blanket gets finished before we give it to [Name]."* The baby will feel loved each time he (or she) uses it. You are helping share God's love with this child. When you see (*Name*) here at church, be sure to stop and talk to (him or her). Let's have a prayer. Will each of you take hold of the blanket as we pray?

Thank you, God, for (*Name*) and that (he or she) is now a part of our church family. We want (*Name*) to know that you love (him or her) and that (he or she) is a very special person. Amen. (*If the blanket is complete, present it to the baby.*)

Delia Halverson

SYMBOLS OF OUR FAITH

Scripture: Deuteronomy 6:4-9
Season/Sunday: Any
Focus: To introduce some of the symbols of Christianity to the children.
Experience: The children will explore the symbols that you have in your place of worship (and/or elsewhere in your church buildings) and relate them to symbols they are familiar with in the community.
Arrangements: Make drawings of symbols around your community (or if preferred, download from the Internet); use symbols for such things as restrooms; handicapped parking, traffic signs, no smoking signs, school crossings, and others. Explore your place of worship for symbols that convey our Christian faith. Choose the explanations below that are appropriate to your congregation.

Leader:	Good morning! I have some drawings that may be familiar to you. What do these mean? (*Hold up one symbol after another for them to identify.*)
Children:	(*Varied responses*)
Leader:	These are symbols that we see around our community. They are like talking with pictures. We have symbols that we use in our church too. Some of them are here in this room, and some are elsewhere in our buildings. Let's look at some of the symbols. (*Ask the children to move with you to the place where some of the symbols are displayed in your worship area. The ones that were brought in or the pictures you took of symbols can*

be explained as you sit together. Be sure to use symbols that you find in the architecture, such as circles, squares, triangles, and arches, as well as those that are obvious.)

- Arch: God is over us as the heavens above.
- Bread/wheat and chalice/grapes: Communion.
- Candle: Christ is the Light of the World.
- Circle: God's eternal love.
- Colors (*seasonal*):
  - Purple (Advent = royalty, getting ready for the King; Lent = penitence, admitting our mistakes)
  - Blue (Advent = hope)
  - White (Christmas and Communion = purity)
  - Green (Epiphany and Ordinary Seasons = growth and outreach)
  - Red (Pentecost = flame of Holy Spirit)
- Cross: Christ died for us and has power over death.
- Dove: Peace or Holy Spirit.
- Flame: Holy Spirit.
- Rainbow: God's covenant with us.
- Square (or anything with four parts): Four Gospels (Matthew, Mark, Luke, John).
- Stained-glass window: The story/message the picture tells.
- Triangle (or anything with three parts): Trinity (God, Jesus, Holy Spirit).
- Water or baptismal font: Washed clean at baptism.

Leader: These are some of the symbols that help us understand more about God and about what we believe. Let's have a prayer and thank God for the symbols of our faith. (*Prayer*)

Delia Halverson

(*The Abingdon Children's Sermon Library, vol. 2*, ed. Brant D. Baker © 2007 by Abingdon Press. Adapted and used by permission.)